Salem Lyceum

Historical Sketch of the Salem Lyceum

With a List of the Officers and Lecturers Since its Formation in 1830

Salem Lyceum

Historical Sketch of the Salem Lyceum
With a List of the Officers and Lecturers Since its Formation in 1830

ISBN/EAN: 9783744736190

Printed in Europe, USA, Canada, Australia, Japan

Cover: Foto ©Suzi / pixelio.de

More available books at **www.hansebooks.com**

HISTORICAL SKETCH

—OF THE—

SALEM LYCEUM,

WITH A LIST OF THE

OFFICERS AND LECTURERS

SINCE ITS FORMATION IN 1830.

AND AN EXTRACT FROM THE

ADDRESS OF GEN. HENRY K. OLIVER,

DELIVERED AT THE OPENING OF THE

Fiftieth Annual Course of Lectures,

NOVEMBER 13th, 1878.

SALEM:
PRESS OF THE SALEM GAZETTE.
1879.

SALEM LYCEUM.

The Salem Lyceum was formed in the month of January, 1830, and the first lecture was delivered on the evening of February 24, of that year, in the Methodist meeting-house in Sewall street, by Judge Daniel A. White. Other similar institutions were organized at about the same time in the principal towns and cities of the country. Of these, the Salem Lyceum and the Concord Lyceum, formed at the same time, alone survive, the others having long since ceased to exist. During these years, fifty successive courses of lectures have been delivered to its members, covering a great variety of topics, engaging the services of many very distinguished persons, and contributing not a little to the social education and entertainment of the public.

The Lyceum, as a specific institution, was an intellectual development of the time of its birth, and, under the name of Institute, flourished in England even before it was transplanted hither. The persons engaged in the formation of the Lyceum in Salem were the principal gentlemen of the town. The first meeting was held at the house of Col. Francis Peabody, (the present residence of John H. Silsbee, Esq., No. 380 Essex street), on Jan. 4th, 1830. It was then,

"Voted, That it is expedient to establish an institution in Salem for the purpose of mutual instruction and rational entertainment, by means of lectures, debates, &c."

A meeting was subsequently held in the Town Hall,

(Jan. 12), when a committee was appointed "to prepare a constitution, and submit the same for inspection to the citizens of Salem."

This committee prepared an address to the public, and a form of constitution, which were left for signatures at the Commercial News Room, the Reading Room of the Charitable Mechanic Association, and at the bookstores.

On the evening of January 18th, 1830, a meeting of the signers of the constitution was held in the parlor of the Essex House, then known as "Pickering Hall," and frequently used for public purposes. At this meeting and at an adjourned meeting, the following officers were elected, and constituted the first Board of Directors:—

President—Daniel A. White.
Vice President—Stephen C. Phillips.
Corresponding Secretary—Charles W. Upham.
Recording Secretary—Stephen P. Webb.
Treasurer—Francis Peabody.
Managers—Rev. William Williams, Caleb Foote, Esq., Rev. Rufus Babcock, Hon. Leverett Saltonstall, Col. Jonathan Webb, Dr. Abel. L. Peirson, Dr. Malthus A. Ward, Dr. George Choate, Hon. Rufus Choate, John Moriarty, Esq.

It was originally intended that public debates should be among the exercises of the Lyceum, and the by-laws provided for the appointment of disputants upon the affirmative and negative sides of such questions as might be discussed. But this plan was never carried out. A course of lectures was, however, started forthwith, and these lectures were mostly delivered by members of the

Lyceum, who contributed their services without fee or reward. Of the lectures in the first course, all but four were delivered by gentlemen of Salem. For several years afterwards the lecturers were many of them residents here, and the fee rarely exceeded ten dollars.

The lectures were at first given in the Methodist Meeting House, in Sewall street. The use of the Town Hall had been asked for, and had been granted by the town; but upon the latter declining to allow permanent seats in the Hall, the Lyceum concluded to go elsewhere. The lectures were afterwards delivered in the Universalist Meeting House. But during the summer of 1830, plans were adopted for the construction of the present Lyceum Hall, and in September a contract was made with William Lummus to build it, and so expeditiously was the work forwarded that it was ready for occupancy in January, 1831. The original cost of the building was $3036.76, and it was erected upon land bought of Mrs. Sarah Orne, for the sum of $750, of which $545 was raised by subscription. The cost of the lectures was so small, and the income of the Lyceum was so large, that in a very few years the debt upon the building was extinguished, and it has since been the property of the members of the Lyceum.

The tickets for the Lyceum were at first sold at Mr. Buffum's bookstore, in Central Building, and afterwards for many years were subscribed for in the anteroom of the hall, where the lists were in charge of Mr. William Mansfield, who for a long period was identified with the Lyceum by his services. Two courses soon became necessary, so great was the demand for tickets, and it was customary to secure a repetition on Wednesday evening of the lecture first delivered on

Tuesday evening. The evening of Tuesday was usually preferred by the Orthodox subscribers, and that of Wednesday by the Unitarians, and hence the audiences became marked in their character in this respect. The selection of evenings was made by drawing "lots," under Mr. Mansfield's direction. Gentlemen's tickets at the outset were sold for $1, and ladies' tickets for 75 cents; but it was not considered proper for ladies to purchase tickets, unless "introduced" by a gentleman. Their tickets therefore ran as follows:—

ADMIT

TO THE

SALEM LYCEUM,

A LADY,

Introduced by

TUESDAY,

B. TUCKER, *Rec. Sec.*

But it is significant of the change that has since occurred in public views of what is proper for females in this respect, that for many years ladies have not only attended the lectures upon equal terms with gentlemen, but have assisted to deliver them, until it has come to be thought that a course is incomplete without a lady lecturer or reader.

During the fifty courses of lectures since the beginning, eight hundred and fifty-three lectures have been delivered before the Lyceum, and it will be noticed by a perusal of the lists which are printed herewith that the names embrace many of those most distinguished in the world of literature, science, and politics. It would probably be impossible to find any other institution in the country which could present such a distinguished list of instructors as this Lyceum.

It ought to be mentioned that, during all these years, the Lyceum has maintained a "free platform," and during recent years especially, nearly all topics of moral, political and social interest, have been discussed with the utmost freedom consistent with the proprieties of such an institution.

In the year 1852, the Lyçeum obtained of the Legislature a new Act of Incorporation, under which it acts at the present time. A perusal of this document will inform the reader of the peculiar character of the institution, and of the privileges and rights of its members.

ADDRESS.

EXTRACT FROM THE ADDRESS DELIVERED BY HON. HENRY K. OLIVER, AT THE OPENING OF THE FIFTIETH ANNUAL COURSE OF LECTURES OF THE SALEM LYCEUM, NOV. 13TH, 1878.

Among the institutions affording popular lectures, is that in which we are now specially interested, our own Lyceum, this evening celebrating its semi-centennial anniversary. The word Lyceum is of Greek origin, and is the name which was given to a gymnasium, or place of physical and mental instruction, outside and easterly from the city of Athens, and where Aristotle taught,—a temple dedicated to "Apollo Lyceus," or "Apollo of the Light," standing close by and originating the epithet. Our English words, "lucidity," "lucent," "lucid," and their relatives, are from the same root. The name is appropriate, for from the Lyceum, or house of light, is to radiate the night-dispelling light of knowledge. There was, at one time, on the ceiling of this hall, just above the stage, a fresco painting of Apollo Lyceus, in his fiery chariot with fiery coursers. It happened that a gentleman, groping one day in the dark of the attic, put his foot, uninvited, into the chariot, and through its bottom, into the hall. So the bright ceiling was removed, and a blind put over the hole. There were, also, on the walls in front, frescos of the orators, Cicero and Demosthenes, and of our then townsmen, Judge White and Joseph Peabody, the father of Col. Francis Peabody. Time and whitewash have obliterated them.

And here, leaving for a while the direct subject before me, let me speak of the extraordinary array of men of note, expert and eminent in almost every department of learning, whom I encountered, on coming here from Boston, a stripling of eighteen years, and with whom it was my very great privilege and benefit to associate for many subsequent years. If the language I use seem to my younger hearers inordinately eulogistic, or exaggerated, I appeal, without fear, to those whose memories recall the men. My limit of time permits me to name but few.

Bear in mind that the population of Salem was then but about 13,000, or one-half of its present number, and mostly confined within the strip of land between the South and North Rivers, now approaching annihilation. But few houses were in North Salem, and none in South beyond the junction of Mill with Lafayette streets, till you reached the Derby estate. Every man of note was known to all his fellow-townsmen, if not personally, yet by name and character. As is known of ancient Athens at its best,—quoting from Hypercides, an oration-writer by profession of those days,—"It is impossible for a man in this city to be of good repute, or otherwise, without all of us knowing it."

And first, I name the venerable and venerated JOHN PRINCE, minister of the First Church, whose advanced years had not weakened his love of science, nor paralyzed the skill of his hands in the construction of instruments of precision and experiment. Herein "his eye was not dimmed, nor his natural force abated." Earth and sky were the fields of his successful investigation,—and he prepared his own means of research,—microscope, telescope, pneumatic-pump, electric and magnetic apparatus, all seeming to come complete from his successful make and manipulation, like Minerva from the brain of Jove, ready for active work, the enthusiasm of youth unweakened by any impotence of years. His house,—that now occupied by David Moore on Federal street,—was at once home, library, lecture-room, workshop, and cabinet of curiosities, a rare and interesting combination of the equipments of science, which I often visited.

Nathaniel Bowditch, whose statue in bronze now marks his resting-place at Mount Auburn, was a marvel of mathematical and scientific attainment. His fame can never die, nor his name cease from the lips of men, till ship and sailors cease to grope their way across trackless seas. A victorious student was he in the severest fields of mathematical contest, making that best use of his triumphs, in their practical utilization and response to the demands of society, and this in such simplicity of appliance and working, that the average mind encounters small difficulty therein. His translation into English of the Celestial Mechanics of Laplace was a most acceptable relief, as it interpolated steps which, though they were needless to the author's marvellous mind, were most embarrassing to the average student, and subjected him to much wearying study to make the connections necessary to the understanding of the subject. Yet though absorption in study is apt to make men recluses, and sometimes even repulsive in manner, the learned halo about them seeming to ordinary men a sort of dense impoundment, no man within my memory was more genial, more communicative, more demonstrative in all the courtesies and ordinary socialities of life. I knew him well, being Librarian at that time of the Salem Athenæum, of which he was President, and coming into contact with him every day.

JOHN PICKERING, (son of the well known Col. Timothy Pickering, of revolutionary work and fame), and in recalling and naming him, there return feelings of most earnest respect and gratitude for many acts of personal kindness and assistance in my inexpert days as a teacher. A man was he justly and widely honored for his large and varied learning, specially in the classic languages and literature, possessing that exact knowledge of details in grammatical laws and verbal construction which aid the young student in many a distressful struggle, as well as give certainty of true scholarship and merited renown to the man himself. Yet he seemed to be wholly unconscious of his own intellectual and scholarly greatness and grasp,—mingling in with us all as a gentle and companionable friend. He was the author,—and all students of Greek blessed him therefor,—who, with the aid of Dr. Daniel Oliver, also of Salem, edited and published a Lexicon of that peerless language with English renderings,—students before that time having to get the meaning of their words through the medium of Latin. His home was on Chestnut street, corner of Pickering street.

I may here mention, as men of scientific and literary note, two relatives of Dr. Daniel Oliver, then resident here, Dr. B. L. OLIVER, and his nephew,—in the law,—of the same name. All three of them were noticeable for their skill in music. It seems to be in the breed. They, and all of the name hereabouts,—including also many in whom the compound name of Oliver-Wendell occurs, were descendants from Surgeon Thos. Oliver, the English immigrant to Boston in 1632, who from the seven generations that have followed, has supplied to Harvard and Dartmouth Colleges, up to 1870, thirty-six out of their forty-five graduates of that name, besides a long roll by marriage into other names, and of these three or four Doctors in each generation. There is a smell of medicine all adown the line.

I next mention JOSEPH STORY, the great jurist and judge, a marvel of legal learning, reinforced by an amount of general attainments and accomplishments, that it would seem might require more than an ordinary life to secure. His powers of conversation, fluency of speech, and command of words, were, like those of Dr. Bentley, of the East Church, the admiration of their day. No subject seemed to be beyond their reach, grasp and control, and they each seemed to be ready with speech and argument for whatever subject-matter might turn up.

I will here mention one, Mr. THOMAS SPENCER, whom, however, I did not meet till about 1825–26, when he came to Salem, having immigrated to the United States from England in 1816, and who, after a long residence here, returned to his own country, where he died, to enjoy in retirement a valuable inherited estate. A hard-working day-laborer while here, as a tallow-chandler, he yet became noted for his knowledge and skill in the science of Optics, and his expertness in arboriculture. He was also the originator of that deservedly famous and toothsome confection, sought by young and old, rich, dainty, and durable in its relish, and which made Salem famous for titbits, as well as for witches, beauty, and learning,—the noted "Gibralter," taking name from its firm make and power of withstanding long continued siege of suck. To my recent gustatory experience, however, the modern is inferior in richness of tonguey tickle and power of endurance to the old. Is its making one of the lost arts?

Mr. Spencer's leaving was matter of great regret, and his frequent letters hither, and his hospitable reception at his English home of American visitors, testified to his grateful memory of his sojourn with us. That truth is stranger than fiction, was verified in a life, which, starting among the zeros of social position and mental opportunity, culminated into that of a wealthy and hospitable land-holder, and of an eminent man of science. The love of learning is of most democratic propensities, taking root and growing in whatever soil, regardless of anything, excepting its geniality, affluence of food, and power of push towards growth and maturity.

But, of these samples, perhaps enough have been quoted. The difficulty is not to find, but, to select, one is so bewildered with the mighty array. Yet there is one other name, to omit which would be doing violence to my own feelings, and be unjust to him and to you. Its utterance never fails to awaken vivid emotions of grateful respect, and to bring to memory one of whom any city might justly be proud. Always devoted to the good of our community, and to effort by word and act towards its enduring welfare, he regarded himself as less than his town and his townsmen, his affection for each being always earnest and demonstrative. The personal attractions of a manly figure and a winning face, were supplemented by a noble nature, nobly developed, with just impartiality in his estimate of men and their motives and actions. Of eminent rank at the bar, and eagerly sought by clients, his professional obligations never excluded his general culture, and he was at once a wise advocate, a safe adviser, an impressive and eloquent speaker, adorning office, refining society, and enriching home with profusest affection. His worshipping nature made him an earnestly religious man, and for years his rich voice gave utterance to his prayerful spirit as he joined in the service of song in public worship. "So well were the elements mixed in him that

> "Nature might stand up
> And say to all the world: This was a man."

A laudable ambition accepted the offices you gave him. You sent him to Congress without his asking, and you made him your first Mayor. It was LEVERETT SALTONSTALL."

Now it would be hardly possible for a community in which were found men like these, and scores of others, their fellows,—the town probably never had so great a proportion of educated men within its limits, old and younger college alumni were here in dozens,—it would be hardly possible not to feel their control, nor to be inspired by their influence. If you move in the sunshine, you will feel its warmth and know its light. If you walk amid roses, you will inhale their perfume.

And so, at last, when "the fulness of time was completed," the seed germinated and the plant appeared above ground.

The first movement in the direction of public lectures, in our vicinity, is credited to the late Col. Francis Peabody, well known and well remembered by many of us. His home was then in the large brick house on Essex street, west of Plummer Hall and the

Athenæum, on whose site stood his father's house, one of our older and most noted merchants. Col. Peabody's tastes were thoroughly scientific, and much in the direction of the mechanics of science. In his day, say from 1826 to the time of his death in 1867, were very many persons in Salem, both competent and inclined to aid and promote his efforts. The first manifestation seems to have been the course before the Essex Lodge of Free Masons, in the winter of 1827.

In 1828, our Salem Charitable Mechanic Association inaugurated a course of lectures for the gratification and instruction of its members and their families, and during the same year Col. Peabody gave a course of free lectures on "Steam, the Steam Engine, and their Utilities," subjects then new and exciting an intense interest, and which were destined to work marvellous revolutions in the world and its ways.

The same gentleman, in conjunction with Jonathan Webb, gave free lectures on Electricity, in the same season of 1828, in Concert, now Phœnix, Hall, at the foot of Central street. These gentlemen were experts in the science, their practical manipulations verifying their theories with convincing instruction, their apparatus being complete and effective in every respect. I knew them both intimately. Col. Peabody, with his ample means generously poured forth, and his earnestness of work, was well reinforced by Mr. Webb, with equal earnestness, energy of purpose, and physical activity. He was an apothecary, his last place of business having been in the brick building opposite Barton Square Church. His was a spirit of great enterprise, a mind exceptionally well cultivated, and a nature most genial and companionable. Indeed, he was the wit of the town, having that quick sense of the ridiculous, that keen vision in its discovery, and that rich power of expressing it in apt and telling language, that never failed to wake us into an uproar of enjoyment. He was a sort of cachinnatory apostle of mirth and good health, often saying that a merry laugh was better than all the medicine in his shop. His bodily health, however, was never equal to his mental vigor and his love of scientific work, and he died at the early age of thirty-seven years, in August, 1832. At the time of his death, he was engaged in the improvement and enlargement of his electric apparatus,—a splendid plate machine, of the largest diameter then made, being then on its passage to him from St. Petersburg. His early leaving us was deeply lamented, no man in the then town being more generally known or more heartily beloved. As an experimental lecturer he had no superior. I well remember how comically he startled a whole audience in this room by the instantaneous explosion by the electric spark of about twenty air pistols, placed about the cornice of this room, each filled with explosive gas and connected together and to the machine by a copper wire. But few of us were in the secret, and the suddenness and big bang of the discharge, the screams and the "Oh mys" of the feminines, the chirruping of the children, and the outspoken "what-in-thunder is that" of the men, and our own loud laugh, made the hall a confused theatre of uproarious merriment. So did the old experiment of sending a sharp shock of electricity through the joined hands of some scores of people, each one of whom really believed he was the first one hit, so synchronous was the blow. But these were merely the curious and amusing manifestations of powers, which now, in their riper development, have revolutionized travel, business, and all inter-communication, as well as very many of our ways of life. And the cry, like that in Macbeth, is, "and still they come,"—the end is not yet, nay, is it not the mere beginning? So amazing, so almost incredible, have been their developments, their manifestations, their influences, that the world is prepared to receive with small surprise any and whatever discoveries and inventions may be awaiting birth.

These exhibitions, and the familiar oral explanations illustrating them, for written lectures and prepared platform essays had not as yet reached the stage, excited greatest interest, and awakened a determinate purpose to secure more and kindred knowledge, and to create a permanent institution for its attainment and wider diffusion.

The methods of these pioneers had been wisely judicious. They had allured, not repelled,—and so had created scores of "Olivers asking for more." They gave the best teaching, inasmuch as it was of the illustrated verities of science, with palpable exhibit of every scientific truth they announced. The ear heard and the eye saw, and when the earnest men who led the work,—and they were among Salem's then best, and her best were among the best of the whole land,—put themselves to the task of elaborating a permanent means of instruction by lectures, they met the sympathetic encouragement and support of the community.

Confining myself to our own institution (the attempt to create a County Lyceum, though pushed by leading minds in Essex County, failing), it appears that a meeting for its initiation was held at the house of Col. Peabody, then on Essex, near Dean street, on the evening of January 4th, 1830. Twenty gentlemen there gathered, of whom fifteen are dead, the five survivors being Messrs. George Wheatland, David Roberts, Wm. P. Endicott, S. P. Webb and Caleb Foote. Two of them are of our ex-Mayors. Of the deceased I quote Daniel A. White, Robert Rantoul, Jr., Warwick Palfray, Stephen C. Phillips and Dr. A. L. Peirson. Of the twelve gentlemen selected on the 12th of January at the Town Hall, to prepare a Constitution and By-laws, only one, Dr. Choate, survives. Among them were Judge White, L. Saltonstall, S. C. Phillips, A. L. Peirson and Col. Peabody. Adopting the motion of Dr. Peirson—whose sad death in 1853, at the terrific railroad disaster at Norwalk Bridge, Conn., is yet fresh in the memory—it was voted, that "it is expedient to establish in Salem an institution for the purpose of mutual instruction and rational entertainment by means of public lectures and debates." This vote took substantial form by an election, on the following 18th of January, of five executive officers; a President, Judge White; a Vice President, Stephen C. Phillips; a Recording Secretary, S. P. Webb; a Corresponding Secretary, Chas. W. Upham; and a Treasurer, Francis Peabody; an admirable selection. At an adjourned meeting on the 20th, the organization was completed by the addition of ten Directors. To the self-sacrificing labors of three of these men, Messrs. White, Phillips and Peabody, this institution owes the deepest gratitude. Their names should be honored by permanent record on its walls.

To those of you who, year after year, during the last half century, have partaken of the wholesome food offered, at cheapest rate, by this institution, and who have come to its feasts as naturally and as regularly as herd and flock seek their pasture, it may seem singularly strange, that its initiation should have encountered opposition. Yet it did—though that antagonism from its very unreasonableness, served the good purpose or augmenting the earnestness and activity of its friends, and their resolve to achieve success. So to those who, after the lapse of a half century therefrom, shall celebrate the establishment here of a Free Public Library, and a free Public Reading Room, whenever such "consummation devoutly to be wished," shall occur, it will seem equally strange, perhaps incredible, that any opposition now, should have delayed an event which is, nevertheless, an inevitable certainty, though many may die without the sight. But returning—the good ship "Lyceum" was now launched, equipped, officered, and ready for sea, and a favoring breeze swelling her canvass, she began her voyage under the very best auspices.

As I recall the men who began this work, all or whom were my companions and friends, there returns the old feeling of profound respect for the noble and unselfish spirit which characterized them. I doubt whether in any community of equal population (we had then about 15,000 people), or in even one of a greater,—such an array of men, so noteworthy, so brilliant, excelling in so great a variety of acquirement, could be found. And yet that array could here have then been doubled and trebled. Four of them were, at different dates, members of Congress, that distinction, at that date, signifying high honor,—four were lawyers, three were clergymen, and five were men in absorbing and responsible business positions. Of the twenty original projectors, fifteen are dead, of the twelve who prepared the Constitution, eleven are dead, of the fifteen who composed the first corps of officers, twelve are dead. And as indicative of the sharp sectarianism that then divided and disturbed the community, it may be mentioned that these officers were selected, not without regard to their several religious beliefs. Eight were of Unitarian, and seven of Orthodox creeds, all the five executive officers being Unitarians, and yet no religious dissonances seem to have marred their doings, nor have any since disturbed the harmony of the institution, or of its management. Science and true learning stand on neutral ground, each bearing a perpetual flag of truce. The whole conducting of this institution has been with the utmost liberality and with unbiased impartiality, in both politics and religion.

The earliest embarrassment encountered, was that of finding a room adapted to meet all the exigencies of varied lecture-work, that of the essayist, and that of the experimental scientist, and, at the same time, convenient to the audience in all respects of seats, of sight, and of hearing. There was no such place, and the best that could be done was to use some one of our churches. The Mechanic Hall, now greatly improved, was not built till ten years later. The Methodist Chapel, in Sewall street, and the Universalist Church, on Rust street, were utilized during the first season, the introductory of February 24th, 1830, by Judge White,—and the second, of March 3d, by Rev. Dr. Brazer,—being delivered in the former, and the remaining twelve in the other two before named. So were the first five of the second course, beginning on the evening of December 1st, 1830,—the sixth of that course being given as the first in this hall, January 20th, 1831, by Hon. Stephen C. Phillips. During the summer of 1830, and in the interval between the first and second course, this hall was erected on a portion of the then garden of Rev. Mr. Upham, then of the First Church, afterwards our Representative in Congress, who occupied the estate now owned by Dr. Cate. The building was planned and reared under the supervision of Col. Peabody. The land was purchased of Mrs. Sarah Orne, recently deceased, for $750, the cost of the building being about $4,500, including fixtures, and the property stands unincumbered. The changes of this year have greatly added to its conveniences. It is in the form of the ancient Roman Theatre, but with its stage carried farther back from the audience. For the purpose of hearers, it is well adapted, though a slight echo occasionally vexes the speaker,—but for advantageous display of illustrative diagrams, and show of tentative apparatus, it is not without objection, inasmuch as the seats on the extreme right and left of the auditorium, afford no clear view of these means of elucidation The funds for its erection were from donations by friends,—the money being advanced by Judge White, whose home was adjoining the City Hall.

His introductory lecture, upon "The Advantages of Knowledge," was a model of classical English, neither stilted nor meretricious in style, nor showy in language—but plain, clear, and forcible, an overflowing fountain of wise thought and well considered practical suggestion. No man in any community could be more earnest and solicitous for the mental and moral welfare of his fellow men, or a more pure example in all that pertains to a good life and to best citizenship. He gave his large and valuable private library to the Essex Institute, at different times, in all eight thousand volumes.

The first lecture in this hall was, as I have said, by Mr. Stephen C. Phillips, upon "the influence of this country and its age upon the condition of mankind." The author was equal to the theme, and the subject, fertile in suggestion and rich in substantial material, was admirably treated, and eloquently delivered. Mr. Phillips, the only son of one of our rich merchants, had graduated with distinction at Harvard in the class of 1819, in which same year Rufus Choate had graduated at Dartmouth. He began life here under most favorable prestige, and with best auguries of success. An excellent scholar, with wide general culture, a fluent and pleasing speaker, he kept the audience in steady and vivid attention, and gave a lively impetus to the new departure. He did not give himself to professional study, but entered upon a commercial life.

Before speaking, as I propose to do, upon other lecturers and their lectures, let me give some statistics of the institution itself. The new hall, concentrating the general interest upon something before unknown in Salem, and now recognized as the specialty of a new means of exceptional instruction and refined amusement, seemed to assure the success of the enterprise, by "giving it a local habitation and a name"—and that assurance has been verified by the continuous and uninterrupted good work of half a century. The hall itself has also afforded convenient facilities for a great variety of gatherings, scientific, political, and musical. Its central situation, facility of access, and general aptness; its form and arrangement, all unite to render it desirable, while the seating is such that everybody can see everybody else.

The Lyceum has presented under its eighteen different Presidents (the term of Dr. Loring, now in its twelfth year, being the longest), 853 lectures, having enlisted in its service men of eminent rank in science and in letters.

I find on its records the names of Daniel Webster, Rufus Choate, Edward Everett, and his kinsman Alex ander H. Everett, Ralph Waldo Emerson, Oliver Wendell Holmes, Charles F. Adams and ex-President John Quincy Adams, Horace Mann, Jared Sparks, James Walker, Robert C. Winthrop, the twins, O. W. B. and B. W. O. Peabody, Caleb Cushing, Henry Giles, Edwin P. Whipple, Wendell Phillips, Charles Sumner, Henry Wilson, James Freeman Clarke, Edward Everett Hale, Louis Agassiz, George William Curtis, Fanny Kemble, James T. Fields, and George Bancroft.

More than a score these, of the most eminent literary celebrities of their day, three of them Presidents of Harvard College and eight of them eminent members of Congress, while any one in the list could better have filled that position than any average member of to-day. Of this list I find that Mr. Emerson was the most frequently employed, having lectured twenty-eight times, and Wendell Phillips appearing sixteen times, Mr. Giles the same number, and James F. Clarke eight times. Of this list, Mr. Emerson, reckoning from the twentieth course, lectured in every course but one for twenty-one years. I doubt whether such continuity can be paralleled in any other Lyceum. In 1848 Prof. Agassiz gave one course of five on the Animal Creation, and in 1849 one course of three on the Vegetable Kingdom. Mr. Giles, in 1842, one course of three on Irish History, Character, and Society. In 1848, J. P. Nichols gave a very instructive series of six, on Astronomy. Of some few of these lectures I will speak farther on.

From the start it was intended to make use, to a considerable extent, of the talent and means of our own citizens, and I find among the names those of Judge White, John Brazer, Francis Peabody, A. L. Peirson, George Choate, Rufus Choate, Thomas Spencer, S. C. Phillips, Henry Colman, H. K. Oliver, Charles W. Upham, Jonathan Webb, John Pickering, Leverett Saltonstall, Caleb Foote, Edwin P. Whipple, George H. Devereux, Charles G. Page, George B. Loring, George W. Briggs, and Octavius B. Frothingham.

Payment for lectures, excepting for stated courses, was not the early rule; the necessary expenses of travel and of moving apparatus only being met. The highest single fee was of $100, to Mr. Webster; the lowest, $10 and $20, to ordinary parties. For lectures by Mr. Evans, repeated on successive evenings in a double course, $100 were paid; and $400 to Mr. Barbour, for a course of nine double lectures on Phrenology. Townsmen, after 1836, seemed to have received $20 a lecture. The employment of special "*stars*," at specially high rates, does not seem to have been encouraged.

Out of the whole number of 853 since the start in 1830, 170, or about one-fifth, have been given by Salemites, and these generally on scientific subjects. Up to 1845, they had given 127. There was then a falling off. Between 1845 and 1853 they gave 14, and in the seven next years, to 1860, but 4; in the following seventeen years 29, the greatest number by any one, and in the earlier courses, being 9, (H. K. Oliver). The concerts, usually at the opening of a course, have been 14 in number, all between 1830 and 1848, and all of exceptional excellence, as were the several exhibitions in Reading and in Declamation. I will now speak of some of the more prominent of the lectures, as I recall them, having already alluded to those by Judge White and S. C. Phillips, and to those of Col. Peabody and Mr. Webb, and I select those by Mr. Emerson, Mr. Upham, Mr. Giles, Mr. Webster, Mr. Hudson, Mr. Whipple, Mr. Catlin, and the scientific lectures of Prof. Agassiz and Prof. Page.

Ralph Waldo Emerson, our most frequent lecturer, was a son of Rev. Wm. Emerson, of Boston, minister of its First Church, which, successively standing on State street, on the Joy's building site, and on Chauncy Place, is now on the Back Bay.

For variety of subject, aptness in treatment, great intellectual display, and profound power of thought, I can imagine nothing superior. It used to be said of him that he was too much of a transcendentalist, prone to discuss subjects transcending the reach of the senses, and so beyond reach of the average comprehension. Of his ability to grapple and to vanquish each and all of those he attempted, there is no lack of proof, while the very fact of his frequent appearance here, shows conclusively that he was never beyond our reach, however high he soared, and that is a compliment to us, and we were never willing to dispense with his teachings. Not seldom were we startled by some new application of an old word to a new use, or of an old word applied felicitously to a new thought, and clothing that thought with new attraction. His lectures that I specially mention, were those on Manners, and on Napoleon, and most impressive and winning of attention were they. To measure them all aright, one would need to be Emerson himself, and I will only venture a word or two about these two. He gave his own conception of fine manners. One meets them, he said, but once or twice in one's whole life. Their charm is that they are not assumed, neither factitious nor fictitious, being of very nature, natural. Concealing nothing, they display their perfectness by their naturalness, illustrated in each act and word—their beautiful nature being more beautiful than any beautiful form or face, this unartful art of good manners being the very finest of the fine arts. Are we now, in family and school and daily life, allowing it to become one of the lost arts?

Bonaparte he characterized as the best known, and most powerful man of the 19th century, thoroughly of the times, timeserving, neither monk nor saint, nor honest man, and, in its true sense not a hero; with no scruple of means in reaching his ends, acting on the Italian proverb, that "if you would succeed, you must not be too good." Catering for the many, he declared his aristocracy to be the rabble, and yet laboring, artfully for that great middle class that was striving after wealth. In him were combined the elements of agitator, radical, destroyer of prescription, subverter of monopolies and abuse. The noble, the rich, and all sleepy conservatives, hated him, and so England, Rome, and Austria, homes of conservatism, aided by despotic

Russia, fought him. His history was alluring, but he was destitute of sentiment, truth and honesty; a boundless liar, an unmatched egotist, who, in his premature old age, on his lonely island of exile, falsified dates and characters, and strove to make history the show of the theatre. To effect his aims, he would steal, drown, poison, or assassinate. In short, after one had penetrated through the mist of power and splendor that enveloped him, he would find that he had not reached a gentleman, but a rogue,—a villain,—a sort of Jupiter Scapin (as the French say), a scampy Jove. Now, I think, that a quiet life, however obscure, of being good and doing good, is vastly preferable to a life, that on review by posterity, receives such an excoriation.

Mr. Emerson's manner and pose of body on the stage, seemed, at first sight, to have an element of formality, something of stately dignity. Yet this impression vanished very soon, and the hearer was won by the look of a cheerful and cheering face, the sound of a firm, distinct, and mellifluous voice, and an outpour in the very best English of most instructive and suggestive thought.

Mr. Upham's lectures, in 1831, on that obscure delusion, the Salem Witchcraft, indicated rare industry and perseverance of research, with impartial well-balanced judgment of historical evidence and traditionary rumor. They became the foundation of his exhaustive work on that strange and most unhappy delusion,—a delusion by no means confined to this part of the world, —a work in which patience and thoroughness of investigation are only equalled by accuracy of detail and attractive literary style and finish. The work has become a standard authority. When delivered here, the several lectures were of great length, yet local interest in the subject, local allusions, and local names and celebrities, and the eminent fitness of treating this special theme near the place of the occurrences, excited a vivid interest, and kept the large audiences in close attention for more than two hours on each evening. By the well-known work, in which they are now united, and by his admirable and accurate biography of Col. Timothy Pickering, our townsman of revolutionary fame, Mr. Upham has attained a well merited renown as an author. He was a member of Congress in 1854, and the Mayor of the city in 1852.

Rufus Choate's lecture, on the "Romance of the Sea," in 1837, a subject for which his birth-place and early associations and impressions well fitted him, was as unique in its title as it was marvellous in its treatment and exposition. Of all his rich and surpassingly beautiful productions, this was foremost, and most eagerly sought. He was born and had been reared mid the sights and the scenes of the "sad sea-wave." He had listened, in boyhood, to its hoarse murmurings, its defiant roar, and its terrific ragings. His imagination, stimulated by all his early associations, teemed with metaphoric allusions to the ocean, its surroundings, and its eventful histories. Nay, the danger was not wanting, at one time, that the sea would gain a hero, and the law lose one of its most brilliant and dazzling gems.

My acquaintance with Mr. Choate began at college, in 1816, and was of that intimate nature which college life always creates, when there are but few to share it. Dartmouth had, at that time, but one hundred and sixteen students, in all its four classes, and he, of the class of 1819, was head and shoulders above every man in all that makes perfection of scholarship and literary finish, yet all unconscious did he seem to be of his own complete eminence. As I have written of him in another place, "my mind's eye often sees his manly and attractive figure and strangely winning face, and my mind's ear often hears his deeply resonant and impressive voice; and there is again wakened many a reminiscence of his gentleness of temper and disposition, his warm sympathies, his innate sense of right, his refined courtesy, his completeness as a gentleman, his love of all that is beautiful in life, in nature, and in art; his wonderful mental gifts, his marvellous memory and acquisition of all varied learning." No man in college was ever named with him in rate of scholarship. In fact, we set him apart and above us all, as on a pedestal by himself, "himself his only parallel." His essays then were best of all, leading us captive by his grasp of subject, his eloquent diction, his beautiful imagery, and charm of profuse illustration, his command of words and skill in their use; and in this "Romance of the Sea," and in his others, "The History of Poland," (1831), and "The applicability of American scenes and history to the genius of Walter Scott," he showed an equal command of his themes, and equal power and attraction in treatment and delivery. But of all his productions, this was the crowning glory. A singular fate befel it; it having been stolen after a delivery in New York, the only consolation for the great loss being that no mortal save himself, or, perhaps, his son Rufus, could possibly decipher it. Like all the rest of his chirography, it was burdened with abbreviations, interlinings, and erasures,—a very labyrinth of hieroglyphics, resembling nothing so much as the tracks on paper of an ink-smeared spider.

From about 1823, Mr. Choate practised law in Peabody, then South Danvers; in 1828, he removed to Salem: and in 1836, to Boston. He represented this district in Congress in 1831 and 1834—two sessions—dying in July, 1859, at Halifax, on his second voyage to Europe. The universality of grief which this event occasioned, expressed the strong hold he had upon all hearts. The pulpit bore witness to his excellence as a man, and his noble moral influence, and the Bar to his great power as a lawyer and an advocate, and a fair and honorable antagonist.

The lecture of Daniel Webster, at the opening of the 8th Course, in 1836, "upon Popular Knowledge as applied to scientific improvements," though in some degree outside and foreign to his habitual studies and pursuits as a lawyer and a statesman, was treated with that comprehensive grasp and command which become the normal function of minds of rarest power, minds which compensate all the many and great deficiencies of early training, by a victorious mastery over the widest range of knowledge. The attention of the audience was riveted to the speaker from the beginning to the end. To be sure it was Webster, in his full development, in his massive and superb presence and quiet self-possession,—with the clear utterance of his rich, deep-toned and musical voice, and his grace of delivery, the outward manifestations of the marvellous intellect within—these all conspiring to hold to an almost breathless listening. The subject was handled in an entirely simple way, no one failing to follow as he showed the real and abiding functions of science to be the inciting of art, to bring the power of the human mind to the aid of the human hand; to promote all convenience, to lighten labor, to mitigate toil by enlarging the domain of the human intellect over the elements of matter, to make those elements submit to human rule, human bidding, and to fullest co-operation in securing human happiness.

I can make but brief allusion to the admirable and instructive lectures of Mr. H. N. Hudson, upon Shakspeare (1845 and 1846), with their energetic style and aphoristic sentences, provocative, every way, to farther study of that marvellous genius who "expanded the reach of the drama beyond all its former limits; developing humanity in its stronger lights and subtler movements in a language more diversified by fancy and passion, than was ever before uttered."

Brief, too, must be my reference to the vivacious and quickening essays of our once townsman, E. P. Whipple, sparkling and crispy, full of richest wit and raciest humor, with sound and discriminating analysis of the subject in hand. Three of them I distinctly recall—one upon "Wit and Humor," one upon the "Ludicrous Side of Life," and one upon the "Literature of Impudence," this last, I venture to say—never attempted by any one else, and in which he gave many a stunning specimen of the sublimest insolence and swagger—felicitous specimens of what the Greek poet Menander, calls the very best provision for a prosperous life.

A few words,—all too few for their merit,—must be given to the lectures of Mr. Henry Giles. They were 14 in number, on eleven different subjects, the three upon Irish History, Character and Society, being (not indeed better than the rest, all were of the highest character, of marked originality and best finish), yet specially striking for their fervid eloquence and intense magnetism, embodying, as they did, in burning words and impassioned utterance, the soul-felt warmth, and the overmastering earnestness of an Irishman proclaiming the wrongs of his country, and pleading her cause before the jury of all the world. To Mr. Giles's moral nature wrong was wrong, and the wrongs suffered by his country at the hand of England, were the wrongest of all wrongs, and he denounced them in words, not like those of Talleyrand, "made to conceal thought," but in words that were the voice of the heart, coming, with no uncertain sound, but in tones intended to brand with infamy the nation that he believed had been to his country a worse foe than Russia to Poland. His other lectures, best remembered by me, (all were given in the seasons between 1843 and 1849,) were those upon Burns, Don Quixote, and Falstaff,—all of which evinced a quick, yet exact insight into the inner thought domain of their several authors, revealing, as it were, an inside view of the working of the brain and of its parturitions, by force of intensest stimulus of the imagination. What would be adequate fee for one such look while the brain of Cervantes was generating Don Quixote, or Shakspeare was in genesis of that mountain of bombast, whom the merry wives of Windsor packed into a buck-basket. Ah! what peals of laughter echoed through this hall as Giles,—himself quickened and inoculating us all with the drollery of his subject, his eyes flashing with merriment, his features all aglow with the jollity of his theme, his very frame in a flutter of excitement,—poured from his eloquent tongue, his matchless delineation of this motley conception of the immortal bard equally at home from fairy to Falstaff, from clown to king. Equally fervid, also, was he in all else he gave us, and I can hardly recall a popular lecturer, who so thoroughly captured his audience and held them enchained to his speech.

But I must not omit mention of the lectures upon the life, manners, and customs, and history of our aboriginal Indians, by George Catlin of Wyoming, and afterwards of Philadelphia, who, in the year 1832, penetrated what was then called the Far West,—the region beyond the Missouri river and the Rocky mountains, and north of the Arkansas, that mainly north of the 40th degree of north latitude, where are now the states of Kansas, Wyoming, Colorado, Utah and Dacotah—and passed eight years with "Lo, the poor Indian", "overcoming", as he says, "all the hazards and privations of a life devoted to the production of a literal delineation of races, rapidly passing away, of a dying people, who have no historians to write their annals; and to perpetuating some monument to the memory of lofty and noble tribes. Indian tribes, in their primitive genuineness, the original, pure, unadulterated article,—not that which by contact with the pale faced stealers of their land-heritage, has been debauched by white men and rotted by whiskey, but as he, the first white man they had seen, found them, honest, hospitable, brave, stoical, crafty, cruel, revengeful, relentless, never knowing fear nor fearing death. He visited eighteen different tribes, speaking nearly as many dialects, and comprising about four hundred thousand souls. A painter by profession and taking with him all necessary apparatus, he brought safely home, three hundred and ten portraits of men and women, in all their variety of costumes, of peace and of war,—and two hundred other paintings of their villages, their wigwams, games, religious-ceremonies, their dances, their ball plays, their buffalo-hunting and other amusements, containing in all over three thousand full-length figures, with an endless collection now known as the Catlin Gallery in Washington. Of their domestic, hunting, and warlike implements,—all these exhaustively illustrating people whose origin is beyond reach, whose early history is unknown, whose tribal and national existence is rapidly expiring by grace of civilized vice and bayonet, and of whom, within the past two hundred and fifty years, twelve millions have gone to fatten the soil, whereon they were born, lived their wild life, and died, and whereon forty-four millions of white men, with the multiform paraphernalia which science and art have supplied, are now developing all the possibilities of the highest civilization. These lectures, delivered orally and affluent in anecdote, were of most absorbing attractiveness liberally illustrated by exhibition on the walls and on the stage, of Indians portraits, costumes, weapons and utensils with paintings representing the strange characteristics of the several tribes visited, and all their peculiar ways and means. The lecturer, at times, appeared in the full dress of the war-dance, armed and equipped for service, and with foot, step, hideous grimace and war whoop, gave impressive ideas of the big Indian's darings and prowess. An enthusiastic advocate of the rights of the red men, his descriptions of savage life, were,—like his pictures,—somewhat highly colored, though, in the main, doubtless true to life while his long familiarity with aboriginal archery, may be a good excuse for his occasional drawing of a "long-bow" in their defence.

Mr. Catlin, in 1844, published these lectures in a

two-volume work, profusely illustrated, and bearing the highest official testimony to their statements. Of the scientific lectures, I can make,—for the lack of time and your patience,—but slight mention. They were not many out of the whole, and were upon Heat, Electricity, Magnetism, Electro-Magnetism, General Physics, Optics, Acoustics, Geology, Astronomy, with special lectures on Solar and Lunar Eclipses, one of these last growing out of the fact that the first graduated class of our then English High School, had, in their senior year, (1830), calculated all the total solar eclipses visible in the United States during the nineteenth century. There was also an entire astronomical course of six lectures, with illustrations, by Prof. Nichol, of Scotland. None of this class seem to have been given since 1850, though the discoveries since then, specially in astronomy, acoustics, and the laws and facts of light and sound, have been nothing short of astounding, and yet they have not, to our general community hereabouts, been made known to any special particularity.

I recall, with more readiness of memory, those of Agassiz, on the Animal and Vegetable Kingdoms; those of Peabody and Webb, already noticed; and those of our then townsman, Prof. Charles Grafton Page, afterwards Examiner in the General Patent Office at Washington, and deceased within a few years, the intimate and beloved friend and co-worker of that great and greatly beloved man, the late Prof. Henry, of the Smithsonian Institution.

The illustrative lectures of Prof. Page, a graduate of our Latin School in 1828, and of Harvard in 1832, on Electricity, Magnetism, Electro-Magnetism, and their practical applications, may be justly ranked as exceptionally interesting, instructive, and suggestive. Meeting him soon after my own coming hither, in 1819, as teacher meets pupil, our intimacy ceased only with his death, in 1868. In general development and acquisition as a scholar, he held higher than the average rank, but the special bent of his mind was always in the direction of scientific subjects, both at school and at college, and he was never content till he had verified scientific deductions by exact experiment.

His greatest discovery, occurring about the same time here (in United States) with that of the same nature with Farraday's in England, yet wholly independent thereof, was that of the wonderful principle in electricity, known as "Electro-Electric Induction." Out of this discovery grew an instrument which Prof. Page greatly improved by later inventions, and which is now unjustly called the Ruhmkorff Coil.

Here, with many thanks for your patient indulgence, I relieve you. It was not possible, even with the apparent liberal allowance of these one hundred pages of manuscript, to be fully faithful to my subject, or exhaustively comprehensive in presenting an educational history of fifty years continuance. What has been written may be some material for him who shall be my successor at your centennial celebration.

Your Lyceum is a fixed institution, and I commend for its motto, Virgil's beautiful line,

"Semper honos nomenque tuum, laudesque manebunt."

"Honor, renown and lasting praise,
Attend thee to thy latest days."

SYLLABUS OF LECTURES.

FIRST COURSE. 1830.

Daniel A. White, Salem—Advantages of Knowledge.

John Brazer, Salem—Authenticity of Ancient Manuscripts.

Francis Peabody, Salem—Steam Engine.

Abel L. Peirson, Salem—Physiology.

George Choate, Salem—Geology.

Thomas Spencer, Salem—Optics.

Charles G. Putnam, Salem—Nervous System.

Thomas Cole, Salem—Astronomy.

Stephen C. Phillips read a lecture written by E. Everett—Workingmen's Party.

Stephen C. Phillips, Salem—Public Education, with a sketch of the origin of public schools in Salem.

Henry Colman, Salem—Human Mind.

Joshua B. Flint—Respiration.

Joshua B. Flint—Circulation of the Blood.

Joshua B. Flint—Digestion.

SECOND COURSE. 1830-31.

Rufus Babcock, Salem—Power of Mind.

Alexander H. Everett—A Review of the Continual Progress in Improvement of Mankind.

Alonzo Potter—Moral Philosophy.

Malthus A. Ward, Salem—Gardening.

Leonard Withington—Historical Probability.

Stephen C. Phillips, Salem—The Influence of the Country and the Age in which we Live, on the Condition of Man, as an Individual, a Member of Society, a Political Agent, and an Intelligent and Moral Being.

Henry K. Oliver, Salem—Pneumatics.

Abel L. Peirson, Salem—Biography of Dr. Jenner, and history of vaccination.

Henry K. Oliver, Salem—Solar Eclipse of 1831.

George Choate, Salem—Climate and its Influence on Organic Life.

Charles W. Upham, Salem, (two lectures)—Witchcraft.

Jonathan Webb, Salem, (two lectures)—Electricity.

Alexander H. Everett, (two lectures)—French Revolution.

Thomas Spencer, Salem—Optical Instruments.

Malthus A. Ward, (two lectures) Salem—Natural History.

Francis Peabody, Salem—Heat.

Stephen P. Webb, Salem—Russian History.

Edward Everett—Political Prospects of Europe.

Benjamin F. Browne, Salem—Zoology.

Rufus Choate, Salem—History of Poland.

THIRD COURSE. 1831-32.

John Pickering, Salem—Beneficial Effects Resulting from Associations for the Diffusion of Knowledge.

Caleb Foote, Salem—History of Printing.

Charles G. Putnam, Salem—Whales and Whaling.

Abel L. Peirson, Salem—History of the Circulation of the Blood.

Henry K Oliver, Salem—Pneumatics.

Milton P. Braman—Popular Superstitions.

J. D. Fisher—Education of the Blind.

Wm. Thorndike—Disadvantages arising from the Multiplication of Books.

Abel L. Peirson, Salem—Advantages arising from the Multiplication of Books.

Henry K. Oliver, Salem—Aerostation.

Leverett Saltonstall, Salem—Early History of Massachusetts.

Charles W. Upham read a lecture written by E. Everett.

Dr. Grigg—Physical Education.

William H. Brooks, Salem—Education of the Five Senses.

Thomas Cole, Salem—Meteorology.

John Pickering, Salem—Alleged Uncertainty of the Law.

W. S. Upton—Law of Wills.

Henry Colman, Salem—Eloquence.

Joseph E. Sprague, Salem—Character and Services of Washington.

John Codman, Salem—Character of Byron.

J. C. Richmond—Present state of Greece.

Daniel A. White, Salem, read a lecture written by E. Everett.

John S. Williams, Salem—Reform Bill.

Leonard Withington—Defects of Female Education.

Abel L. Peirson, Salem—Spasmodic Cholera.

Alexander H. Everett—U. S. Constitution.

FOURTH COURSE. 1832-33.

Rufus Choate, Salem—Applicability of American Scenes and History to the performances and genius of Sir Walter Scott.

W. H. Brooks, Salem—Advantages of Commerce, with sketches of its history as connected with Salem.

William Sullivan—On the Rules of Evidence as Applied to Common Life.

George S. Hillard—Comparison of Ancient and Modern Literature.

Caleb Foote, Salem—Value of the Union and Consequences of Disunion.

James W. Thompson, Salem—Connexion of Literature with Morality.

R. D. Mussey—Anatomy of the Chest and Spine.

Samuel Worcester—Indian Eloquence.

James Walker—Phrenology.

M. S. Perry—Diseases peculiar to the different classes of society.

Nathaniel West, Jr., Salem—Imprisonment for Debt.

George H. Devereux, Salem—Feudal Ages.

Amos D. Wheeler—Geology.

Samuel G. Howe—Education of the Blind.
Lowell Mason—Science of Music.
Nehemiah Cleaveland—Poetry.
John Farrar—Advantages of Knowledge.
Joshua H. Ward, Salem—History of Spain.
Rufus Babcock, Salem—Moral Nature of Man.
Thomas Spencer, Salem—History of India.
William B. Calhoun—Political Economy.

FIFTH COURSE. 1833-34.

Edward Everett—Agriculture.
E. Evans, (four lectures)—Geography, Manners and Customs of various Countries.
Dr. Barber, (nine lectures)—Phrenology.
George H. Devereux, Salem—Adaptation of Philosophy to the Wants and Condition of Man.
David Merritt, Salem—History of the Jews.
J. V. C. Smith—Mechanism of the Eye.
Charles G. Page, Salem—Pneumatics.
Charles G. Page, Salem—Acoustics.
Charles A. Andrew, Salem.
Stephen P. Webb, Salem—History of Turkey.
Lemuel Willis, Salem—Progress of Society.

SIXTH COURSE. 1834-35.

Caleb Cushing—Education.
Alexander H. Everett—English and American Literature.
George B. Cheever, Salem—Samuel T. Coleridge.
H. McMurtrie, (twelve lectures)—Zoology.
Abel L. Peirson, Salem—Qualifications and Duties of a Physician.
John W. Browne, Salem—Theatre.
Charles T. Jackson—Volcanoes.
George S. Hillard—Americanism.

SEVENTH COURSE. 1835-36.

James Flint, Salem—Poem, Change.

Sylvester Graham—Capabilities of the human frame in respect to the duration of life.

W. B. O. Peabody—Hebrew Commonwealth.

Samuel M. Worcester, Salem—James Otis and Patrick Henry.

B. B. Thatcher—Boston Tea Party.

O. W. B. Peabody—British Poetry during the latter part of the last century.

Leonard Withington—Dangers of Republicanism.

George Putnam—Water.

Jeremiah Smith—Washington.

John Appleton—Sir Humphrey Davy.

William H. Simmons—Education.

Charles C. Emerson—Socrates.

Abel L. Peirson, Salem—St. Peter's Cathedral.

George S. Hillard—Living too fast.

Jonathan F. Worcester, Salem—China.

A. M. Quimby—Electricity.

Ralph Waldo Emerson—Martin Luther.

William Silsbee, Salem—Study of the Beautiful.

B. B. Thatcher—Philosophy of Self-Education.

Henry R. Cleveland—Pompeii.

Charles G. Page, Salem—Heat.

Charles T. Brooks, Salem—Character.

EIGHTH COURSE. 1836-37.

Daniel Webster—Popular Knowledge as applied to Scientific Improvements.

W. B. O. Peabody—Birds.

Horatio Robinson, Salem.

Stephen C. Phillips, Salem—South Sea Expedition.

Nehemiah Adams, Salem—Universal Empire.

Charles G. Page, Salem—Electricity.

Charles G. Page, Salem—Galvanism.

Elisha Bartlett—Application of Science to Common Life.

William M. Rogers—Egyptian Hieroglyphics and their Bearing upon Revelation.

Samuel M. Worcester, Salem—English Language.

Charles G. Page, Salem—Galvanism.

David Roberts, Salem—Franklin.

William H. Brooks, Salem—French Civil Wars of the 16th Century.

H. R. Cleveland—Spirit and Institutions of the Middle Ages.

Charles G. Page, Salem—Electro Magnetism.

O. W. B. Peabody—English Poets of the Present Century

James W. Thompson, Salem—Sir Walter Raleigh.

John C. Park—Education for the World.

Alexander Young—Pequod War.

Ralph Waldo Emerson—Philosophy of History.

Rufus Choate—Literature of the Sea.

NINTH COURSE. 1837-38.

Horace Mann—Education.

George S. Hillard—Books.

John S. Williams, Salem—Ireland.

John W. Browne, Salem—War.

Leonard Withington—"The Light which the Theory of our Government Sheds on the Practice of its Citizens."

W. B. O. Peabody—Hebrew Commonwealth.

H. R. Cleveland—The Superstitions of the Classic Ages.

Jones Very, Salem—Epic Poetry.

Thomas Spencer, Salem—The Vegetation of Salem and Vicinity.

William M. Rogers—Ross's Expedition to the Polar Seas.

Samuel M. Worcester, Salem—Irish Eloquence.

James C. Alvord—The Mutual Relations and Influences of the Various Occupations of Life.

Oliver Wendell Holmes—English Versification.

Abel L. Peirson, Salem—Animal Magnetism.

M. Mariotti—Marie Louise, the Widow of Napoleon.

William Lincoln—The French Neutrals of Nova Scotia.

James Walker—Transcendentalism.

An Exhibition by Pupils from the N. E. Institution for the Blind.

O. W. B. Peabody—English Female Writers of the Last Century.

John P. Cleveland—Ancient History of Michigan.

George Bancroft—The Capacity of the Human Mind for Culture and Improvement.

Henry Ware, Jr.—The Poetry of Mathematics.

John Lewis Russell, Salem—Geology.

TENTH COURSE. 1838-39.

George Catlin, six lectures on the Character, Customs, Costumes, &c., of the North American Indians.

Jared Sparks—Causes of the American Revolution.

Hubbard Winslow—The Sun.

C. H. Brewster—The Sources of National Wealth.

Charles T. Torrey, Salem—Common School Education.

Ephraim Peabody—The Capacity of the Human Mind for Culture and Improvement.

Henry K. Oliver, Salem—The Honey Bee.

Robert C. Winthrop—Popular Education.

Professor Adams—Geology.

Simon Greenleaf—The Legal Rights of Women.

Henry Ware, Jr.—Instinct.

Joshua H. Ward, Salem—Life of Mohammed.

Henry W. Kinsman—Life and Times of Oliver Cromwell.

Abel L. Peirson, Salem—Memoirs of Count Rumford.

Converse Francis—The Practical Man.

John Lewis Russell, Salem—The Poetry of Natural History,

John Wayland, Salem—The Progress of Democracy.

Alexander H. Everett—The Discovery of America by the Northmen.

Samuel Osgood—The Satanic School of Literature and its Reform.

Horace Mann—The Education of Children.

ELEVENTH COURSE. 1839-40.

The Oratorio of Joseph and His Brethren, by the Boston Musical Institute.

Orville Dewey—Human Progress.

Andrew P. Peabody—Influence of the Bible on the Sciences, Poetry, and the Fine Arts.

Leonard Withington—Phariseeism.

Converse Francis—The Huguenots or French Protestants in America.

George E. Ellis—The Persecution of the Quakers.

J. S. C. Abbott—Russia.

John L. Hayes—Volcanic Agency.

J. Francis Tuckerman, Salem—Life and Genius of Beethoven.

Oliver Wendell Holmes—National Prejudices.

J. S. C. Abbot—Louis Philippe.

B. B. Thatcher read the lecture by Gov. Everett introductory to the course before the "Lowell Institute" of Boston.

James W. Thompson, Salem—The Conditions of a Healthful Literature.

Thomas B. Fox—Education of the Eye.

Charles Francis Adams—The Influence of Domestic Manners on the American Revolution.

Ralph Waldo Emerson—Analysis, the Characteristic of the Present Age.

Henry Ware, Jr.—The Biography of the Globe.

Henry W. Kinsman.—The Institution of Chivalry and its Influence on Society.

Edward Hitchcock—The Wonders of Science Compared with the Wonders of Romance.

John G. Palfrey—The Siege and Capture of Louisburg.

TWELFTH COURSE. 1840-41.

John Quincy Adams—Faith.

William H. Simmons—Hamlet.

George H. Devereux, Salem—Public Opinion.

John L. Hayes—Life of Cuvier.

William H. Simmons—Macbeth.

Converse Francis—Lessons of the Past.

William M. Rogers—A Business Life.

Heman Humphrey—Mental Philosophy.

Henry K. Oliver, Salem, (two lectures)—The Druids.

Samuel M. Worcester, Salem—Reasoning.

James T. Austin—Siege of Boston.

William G. Swett—Reading.

Samuel Osgood—State and Prospects of the Jews.

Andrew P. Peabody—The Poor Man.

John C. Park—The Law of Marriage.

Richard H. Dana, Jr.—Importance of Cultivating the Affections.

J. V. C. Smith—Ancient and Modern History of the Coinage of Metals.

Ezra S. Gannett—Excitability of the American Character.

THIRTEENTH COURSE. 1841-42.

Henry Giles—Crabbe.

G. Tochman—Poland.

George E Ellis—Scenery of Switzerland.

David H. Barlow—Our Times.

Henry Giles, (three lectures)—Irish History, Irish Character, Irish Society.

Joseph R. Chandler—Cultivation of the Affections as a Means of Happiness.

Nehemiah Adams—Sketches of Nature and Art in Foreign Travel.

John Pierpont—Snow.

Richard H. Dana, Jr.—Macbeth.

Andrew P. Peabody—Fiction.

Daniel Kimball—Whale Fisheries.

Prof. Adam, (two lectures)—Chinese War.

Henry Giles—Burns.

John Lord, (three lectures)—Causes of Modern Civilization.

Oliver Wendell Holmes—Homœopathy.

Richard H. Dana, Jr.—Reality of the Sea.

FOURTEENTH COURSE. 1842-43.

John Quincy Adams—Government.

William Mitchell, (two lectures)—Astronomy, Comets.

Humphrey Moore—March of Mind.

George B. Cheever—Gothic Architecture.

L. F. Tasistro—Master Spirits of English Poetry.

Benjamin Sears—Germany.

Charles Francis Adams, (two lectures)—Shakspeare.

Dr. Fitch—Music as a Fine Art.

Henry Giles, (two lectures)—Byron.

George Bancroft—Spirit of the Age.

Richard H. Dana, Jr.—Woman.

James E. Murdock—Human Voice, with Illustrations.

Edwin Jocelyn, Salem—Spirit of Teaching.

Richard H. Dana, Jr.—Desdemona.

John C. Park—Character of the Pilgrims.

George H. Colton—American Indians.

James E. Murdock—The Passions.

Henry Giles—Elliott, the Corn Law Rhymer.

FIFTEENTH COURSE. 1843-44.

Henry Giles—Life and Writings of Oliver Goldsmith.

Orestes A. Brownson—Dangers of our Present Form of Government.

Gideon F. Barstow, Salem—Poetry and Song.

W. B. O. Peabody—Anglo-Saxon Race.

Ephraim Peabody—Progress of Physical Science since landing of the Pilgrims.

Warren Burton, Salem—Scenery.

Alonzo Gray, (two lectures)—The Chemical Forces; Oxygen, its Agency and Uses.

Henry Giles, (two lectures)—Falstaff; O'Connell, the Irish Agitator.

George Putnam—What is Light.

Ralph Waldo Emerson—The New England Man.
Alfred A. Abbott—Shelley the Poet.
Charles Francis Adams—Milton.
George E. Ellis—What is Known and what is Unknown in the World.
Jonathan F. Stearns—Advantages of a Liberal Education.
Wendell Phillips—The Lost Arts.
Edwin P. Whipple—The Leading Poets, as Wordsworth, Byron, Shelley, &c.
Henry W. Bellows—False Education.
Ralph Waldo Emerson—Want of Distinctive National Character.
Thomas P. Field—Past Prose Writers.

SIXTEENTH COURSE. 1844-45.

Edwin P. Whipple—Literature of Impudence.
David P. Page—Injustice of History to the Common People.
Jason Whitman—The American Citizenship, Responsibilities, &c.
Alonzo Gray—Aqueous Causes of Change.
Wendell Phillips—Influence of Commerce on Personal Freedom.
Ralph Waldo Emerson—The Genius of the New Englander.
John G. Palfrey—History of Massachusetts Colony.
Edwin P. Whipple—Novel and Novelists, (Dickens) and a Poem.
Theodore Parker—Signs of the Times.
Henry W. Bellows—The Pursuit of Truth.
Andrew P. Peabody—The Importance of a Fixed Profession.
Ezra S. Gannett—American Life.
George E. Ellis—Rome.
Theodore Parker—Roman Slavery.
Caleb Stetson—The Useful and Beautiful.
Orestes A. Brownson—Social Reform.
Gideon F. Barstow, Salem—Beranger.
Robert Baird—Characters of the Reigning Sovereigns of Europe.

Samuel M. Worcester, Salem—The Maccabees.

Mrs. Henry Lemon, Salem—Concert.

SEVENTEENTH COURSE. 1845-46.

H. N. Hudson—King Lear, (Shakspeare).

William H. Channing—The College, the Church, and the State.

E. Darling—Chemistry, including Solidification of Carbonic Acid Gas.

W. B. Sprague—Life of Wilberforce.

Stephen Pearl Andrews—Phonography.

George H. Devereux, Salem—Man.

Charles T. Brooks—Omnipresence of the Poetic.

James T. Fields—Books.

A. F. Boyle—Phonography.

Caleb Stetson—Individuality of Man.

Lieut. Halleck—The Battle of Waterloo.

Amory Holbrook, Salem—Galileo.

Samuel Osgood—Rousseau.

Charles B. Haddock—Cultivation of a Taste for Letters by Men of Business.

Fletcher Webster, (two lectures)—China.

Edwin P. Whipple—Wit and Humor.

Theodore Parker—The Progress of Man.

Asa Gray, (two lectures)—Geographical Botany.

Thomas D. Anderson—Reverence for our Government and Laws.

Ralph Waldo Emerson—Napoleon Bonaparte.

EIGHTEENTH COURSE. 1846-47.

Joseph R. Ingersoll—Development.

Edwin P. Whipple—Ludicrous Side of Life.

John S. Dwight—Music.

Thomas Hill—Teachings of Outward Nature.

David H Barlow—Swedenborg.

H. N. Hudson—Desdemona and the Moor.

Thomas T. Stone, Salem—George Fox.
Jared Sparks—American Revolution.
Lorenzo Sabine, (three lectures)—American Loyalists.
Mark Hopkins—Voluntary and Involuntary Powers of Man.
Brown Emerson, Salem—Tour in England.
C. B. Haddock—Novels.
Samuel Johnson, Jr., Salem—Poor of England.
Washington Very, Salem—The Jesuits.
Anson Burlingame—Mexico.
Samuel Elliott—American Liberty.
Ralph Waldo Emerson—Eloquence.
Charles Sumner—Algerine Slavery.
Anson Burlingame—Mexico.
Tremont Vocalists—Concert.

NINETEENTH COURSE. 1847-48

Ephraim Peabody—Religious Tendencies of Modern Science.
Peleg W. Chandler—The Truly Practical Man.
Epes Sargent—Toleration.
Fletcher Webster—India.
J. P. Nichol (two lectures)—Astronomy.
Henry B. Smith—Art.
Alonzo Potter—The Divine Existence.
J. P. Nichol, (two lectures)—Astronomy.
Mark Hopkins—Language.
J. P. Nichol, (two lectures)—Astronomy.
Octavius B. Frothingham, Salem—Bishop Berkley.
William Hincks—Fruits.
Orin Fowler—Cotton Manufactures.
George R. Crockett—Tyranny of Public Opinion.
George H. Devereux, Salem—The Forests of Maine.
Louis Agassiz, (four lectures)—The Animal Creation.
Louis Agassiz, (two lectures)—The Glaciers.

TWENTIETH COURSE. 1848-49.

Daniel Webster—History of the Constitution of the United States; and

James T. Fields—A Poem, "Post of Honor."
Henry D. Thoreau—Student Life in New England, its Economy.
Henry Colman—Philanthropic Institutions of England.
John S. Holmes—Self-Possession.
Louis Agassiz, (three lectures)—Vegetable Kingdom.
Edwin P. Whipple—Genius.
Theodore Parker—Transcendentalism.
Ralph Waldo Emerson—England and the English.
Charles Sumner—Law of Progress.
Edwin P. Whipple—Authors.
Samuel Osgood—Poetry of Mechanism.
Henry Colman—A Conversation about England.
Henry Giles—Don Quixote, Woman.
Henry D. Thoreau—Student Life, its Aims and Employments.
Henry Giles—European Revolutions.
Henry Giles—Don Quixote, Human Life.
Horace Mann, (two lectures)—Knowledge.

TWENTY-FIRST COURSE. 1849-50.

Milton P. Braman—Advantages of Popular Suffrage.
Russell Lant Carpenter—Iceland.
Horace Mann—Thoughts for Young Men.
Sylvester Judd, Jr.—Dramatic Element in the Bible.
E. L. Magoun—Patriotism of Paul.
Alonzo Potter—Spirit of the Age.
Leonard Withington—Evils of Modern Civilization.
Edwin P. Whipple—Character.
Andrew P. Peabody—Moral and Material Worlds.
George H. Devereux, Salem—Progress of Mankind.
Wendell Phillips—Method of Reform.
George Vandenhoff—Readings from the Poets.
R. C. Waterson—Art and Art Unions.
Frances Anne Kemble—"Midsummer Night's Dream.'
Thomas Starr King—Thought and Life.

Theodore Parker—Educated Classes.
Ralph Waldo Emerson—Traits of the Times.
George Vandenhoff—Readings from Shakespeare.

TWENTY-SECOND COURSE. 1850-51.

G. P. R. James—Early History of the Anglo Saxons.
James M. Hoppin, Salem—Egyptian, Grecian and Roman Architecture.
Thomas Wentworth Higginson—Man and Nature.
George Vandenhoff—Readings from Sheridan.
J. D. Butler—St. Peter's Church in Rome.
Israel E. Dwinell, Salem—Intensity a Characteristic of Modern Civilization.
J. W. Taverner—Hood and Ingoldsby, with Readings.
Theodore Parker—The False and True Idea of the Gentleman.
Thomas Starr King—Socrates.
Sylvester Judd, Jr.—Origin of Human Language.
Edwin P. Whipple—The American Mind.
Ralph Waldo Emerson—The Law of Success.
George Shepard—Reading.
Leonard Woods—Democracies of Greece and Rome.
George Thompson—Reforms in England.
O. M. Mitchell—Astronomy.
Caleb Cushing—India.
Edwin H. Chapin—The Actual and Real.

TWENTY-THIRD COURSE. 1851-52.

FIRST SERIES.

Germania Musical Society—Concert.
H. N. Hudson—Falstaff.
Thomas Wentworth Higginson—Mahommed.
John Neal—Pilgrim Fathers.
W. P. Atkinson—Chaucer.
Sylvester Judd, Jr.—Use of the Beautiful.

J. W. Taverner—Readings from Shakespeare.
Ezra S. Gannett—New England and her Institutions.
George W. Briggs, Salem—George Fox.
Charles E. Norton—Life in India as seen at Madras.
A. L. Stone—Kossuth.
Edwin P. Whipple—The English Mind.
H. F. Harrington—Principle of Immortality.
George Shepard—Dean Swift.
James M. Hoppin, Salem—Sketches in Germany.
J. V. C. Smith—Palestine.
Calvin E. Stowe—The West before the Introduction of Steam.
Thomas Starr King—Substance and Show.
Ralph Waldo Emerson—Economy.

SECOND SERIES.

Germania Musical Society—Concert.
H. N. Hudson—The Baconian Method.
Thomas Wentworth Higginson—Mahommed.
John Neal—Law and Lawyers.
W. P. Atkinson—Plea for Poverty.
Sylvester Judd, Jr.—Use of the Beautiful.
J. W. Taverner—Readings from Shakespeare.
Ezra S. Gannett—New England and her Institutions.
George W. Briggs, Salem—George Fox.
Charles E. Norton—Life in India as seen at Madras.
A. L. Stone—Kossuth.
Edwin P. Whipple—The English Mind.
H. F. Harrington—Presence and Absence of Mind.
George Shepard—Charles James Fox.
James M. Hoppin, Salem—German Music.
J. V. C. Smith—Palestine.
Calvin E. Stowe—The West before the Introduction of Steam
Thomas Starr King—Substance and Show.
Ralph Waldo Emerson—Fate.

TWENTY-FOURTH COURSE. 1852-53.

FIRST SERIES.

Germania Musical Society—Concert.
Horace Mann, (two lectures)—Woman.
John A. Dix—Political and Social Development.
Thomas Starr King—Mountains and their Uses.
Eleazer Lord—Improvement of Society.
Charles H. Davis—Astronomical Prediction.
A. A. Miner—Music and Morals.
John L. Russell, Salem—Love of the Beautiful and its Culture.
Oliver Wendell Holmes—Lyceums and Lyceum Lecturers.
Alfred Bunn—Anecdotes of the Stage.
Thomas Chase—Early English Literature.
George Shepard—Demosthenes.
James T. Fields.
Richard H. Dana, Jr.—Edmund Burke.
J. C. Bodwell.
Samuel K. Lothrop—Have we a Bourbon amongst us?
Dexter Clapp, Salem.

SECOND SERIES.

An exact repetition of the above.

TWENTY-FIFTH COURSE. 1853-54.

Mendelssohn Quintette Club—Concert.
George Sumner—France.
Ralph Waldo Emerson—American Character.
George B. Cheever—Reading with reference to Mental Culture.
W. H. Hurlbut—Cuba and the Cubans.
William R. Alger—Peter the Great.
John P. Hale—Last Gladiatorial Exhibition at Rome.
Octavius B. Frothingham, Salem—Europe.
Thomas Starr King—Property.
George W. Curtis—Young America.

Henry Ward Beecher—Ministrations of the Beautiful.

Theodore Parker—The Function of the Beautiful in Human Development.

Bayard Taylor—The Arabs.

Henry W. Bellows—New England Festivals.

Anson Burlingame—The Valley of the Mississippi.

D. A. Wasson—Independence of Character.

Prof. Guyot—Distribution of the Races.

Wendell Phillips—The Lost Arts.

TWENTY-SIXTH COURSE. 1854-55.

FIRST SERIES.

Germania Serenade Band—Concert.

Joseph P. Thompson—Constantinople.

Josiah Quincy, Jr.—Sectional Prejudices.

Thomas W. Higginson—The Old Puritan Clergyman.

Reignold Solger—The present state of the Eastern Question.

Thomas Russell—Influence of Character on National Destiny.

George F. Simmons—The Eastern War.

W. H. Hurlbut—The Middle Ages.

Charles L. Brace—The Principalities of Europe.

Henry Ward Beecher—Patriotism.

Thomas T. Stone, Salem—Rise and Fall of the Roman Empire.

John Pierpont—Education.

Theodore Parker—The Anglo Saxon.

George W. Curtis—Success.

George R. Russell—The Politician.

W. H. Ryder—Ancient and Modern Civilization.

R. C. Waterson—Switzerland.

James Russell Lowell—Edmund Spenser.

Ralph Waldo Emerson—Fruits of English Civilization.

Richard H. Dana, Jr.—Sources of Influence.

SECOND SERIES.

Germania Serenade Band—Concert.
Joseph P. Thompson—Jerusalem and Damascus.
Josiah Quincy, Jr.—Sectional Prejudices.
Thomas W. Higginson—The Old Puritan Clergyman.
Louis Agassiz—The Animal Kingdom.
Reignold Solger—The present state of the Eastern Question.
George F. Simmons—The Eastern War.
W. H. Hurlbut—The Middle Ages.
Charles L. Brace—Ragged Schools.
Henry Ward Beecher—Patriotism.
Thomas T. Stone, Salem—Peasants' War in Germany.
John Pierpont—Moral Influence of Physical Science.
Theodore Parker—The Condition, Character and Prospects of America.
George W. Curtis—Success.
George R. Russell—The Politician.
W. H. Ryder—Ancient and Modern Civilization.
R. C. Waterson—Switzerland.
James Russell Lowell—Analysis of Poetry.
Ralph Waldo Emerson—French Character.
Richard H. Dana, Jr.—Sources of Influence.

TWENTY-SEVENTH COURSE. 1855-56.

FIRST SERIES.

Quartette Club—Concert.
John P. Hale—Trial by Jury.
Mark Trafton—Relation of the Moral to the Intellectual Nature.
James Freeman Clarke—Public Speaking.
J. C. Richmond—War in the East.
Samuel J. May—Magna Charta of New York.
Ralph Waldo Emerson—Beauty.
Octavius B. Frothingham, Salem—Carlo Borromeo.
Reignold Solger—Woman and her Home.

Theodore Parker—Relation of Productive Industry to Social Progress.

Park Benjamin—Age of Gold—a Poem.

G. Gajani—Pius IX. and his flight from Rome.

Wyzeman Marshall—Dramatic Readings.

F. D. Huntington—Common Sense.

William Elder—Relation of Government to Labor.

Ezra S. Gannett—Individuality.

SECOND SERIES.

Quartette Club—Concert.

John P. Hale—Trial by Jury.

Mark Trafton—Relation of the Moral to the Intellectual Nature.

E. H. Sears—Genius.

J. C. Richmond—War in the East.

Samuel J. May—Magna Charta of New York.

Ralph Waldo Emerson—Beauty.

Octavius B. Frothingham, Salem—Carlo Borromeo.

Reignold Solger—Woman and her Home.

Theodore Parker—Relation of Productive Industry to Social Progress.

Park Benjamin—Age of Gold—a Poem.

G. Gajani—Pius IX. and his flight from Rome.

Wyzeman Marshall—Dramatic Readings.

F. D. Huntington—Common Sense.

William Elder—Studies in Mental Philosophy.

Ezra S. Gannett—Individuality.

TWENTY-EIGHTH COURSE. 1856–57.

W. B. Rogers, (three lectures)—Geology.

Edwin H. Chapin—Modern Chivalry.

Samuel J. May—The formula of Social Progress.

J. G. Hoyt—Popular Fallacies.

Moncure D. Conway—Man and his Speech.

William Elder—Natural History of Civilization.

Reignold Solger—The Protestant Character.

E. H. Sears—The Age of Shams.

Octavius B. Frothingham—Epicurus the Philosopher of the World.

Theodore Parker—Benjamin Franklin.

Isaac I. Hayes—Greenland and the Greenlanders.

Ralph Waldo Emerson—Works and Days.

W. B. Hayden—Dignity of Employment.

James Russell Lowell—Dante.

Mendelssohn Quintette Club—Concert.

TWENTY-NINTH COURSE. 1857-58.

Gilmore's Salem Band—Concert.

Henry W. Bellows—Unities of Modes of Education.

G. B. Fontana—King Bomba, or the Sicilian Revolution in 1848.

E. G. Parker—The American Culture of a Love of Reading.

J. G. Hoyt—Popular Education.

James Freeman Clarke—The Yankee.

Wendell Phillips—Toussaint L'Ouverture.

William R. Alger—Life as a Fine Art.

Edwin P. Whipple—Joan of Arc.

E. H. Sears—The Anglo Saxon Element in American Civilization.

Ralph Waldo Emerson—The Finer Relations of Man to Nature.

George B. Cheever—Conscience of the People the Basis of Law.

Theodore Parker—Opportunities of America for aiding Human Progress.

Stephen P. Webb, Salem—The Vigilance Committee of San Francisco.

J. P. Fletcher—Brazil.

Frederic H. Hedge—Private Life in the Dark Ages.

THIRTIETH COURSE. 1858-59.

Henry Ward Beecher—The Law of Sympathy and Repulsion, as applied to Common Life.

John Todd—Three Experiments of Free Government.

James Freeman Clarke—Woman.

George Sumner—European Schools.

Ralph Waldo Emerson—The Conduct of Life.

William R. Alger—Similitudes of Human Life.

Octavius B. Frothingham—The Conservative.

Thomas M. Clark—Public Opinion.

Charles A. Phelps—William Pitt.

Frank P. Blair, Jr.—Destiny of Races on the American Continent.

Edwin P. Whipple—Shakespeare's Method of Characterization.

Edwin H. Chapin—Social Forces.

W. W. Silvester—Readings.

THIRTY-FIRST COURSE. 1859-60.

George Sumner—Lessons from Spain.

Mrs. Sara J. Lippincott—The Heroic in Common Life.

W. W. Silvester—Readings.

Carl Schurz—French Revolution of 1848.

Thomas M. Clark.

W. A. Norton—The Comet of 1858.

Albert G. Browne, Jr., Salem—Utah and the Mormons.

Ralph Waldo Emerson—Manners.

Henry Ward Beecher—The Head and the Heart.

Thomas W. Higginson—Physical Education.

Andrew L. Stone—At Home and Abroad.

Wendell Phillips—Law and Lawyers.

THIRTY-SECOND COURSE. 18 0-61.

Henry Ward Beecher—Young America.

Charles Sumner—Lafayette.

Thomas W. Higginson—American Aristocracy.

Ralph Waldo Emerson—Clubs.

George W. Curtis—Policy of Honesty.

Edwin H. Chapin—Man and his Work.

Edwin P. Whipple—Grit.

Joseph P. Thompson—Tribes of Lebanon and the Druse War.

Henry Giles—Temper.

E. L. Youmans—Chemistry of the Sunbeam.

James M. Hoppin, Salem—Visit to England.

Mr. and Mrs. E. L. Davenport—Select Readings.

THIRTY-THIRD COURSE. 1861-62.

Charles Sumner—The Rebellion.

Ralph Waldo Emerson—Old Age.

Charles F. Brown (Artemus Ward)—The Children in the Wood.

Henry Ward Beecher—The Camp and the Country.

Jacob M. Manning.

Samuel Johnson, Salem—Florence.

John B. Gough—London.

Edward L. Youmans—Man and the Universe.

Edward L. Youmans—Ancient and Modern Science.

Wendell Phillips—The Times.

George H. Hepworth—The Reformer.

Edwin H. Chapin—Elements of National Life.

THIRTY-FOURTH COURSE. 1862-63.

John B. Gough—Here and There in Britain.

Ralph Waldo Emerson—Perpetual Forces.

Wendell Phillips—The Present War.

Theodore Tilton—State of the Country.

George W. Curtis—Thackeray.

Moncure D. Conway—A Leaf from the History of To-day.

Henry Ward Beecher—What shall be done with New England.

Henry Giles—The Complications of War.

Mendelssohn Quintette Club—Concert.

James Freeman Clarke.
S. R. Calthrop—England and America.
Samuel Johnson, Salem—The War and Slavery.

THIRTY-FIFTH COURSE. 1863-64.

John B. Gough—Peculiar People.
Charles C. Coffin—Battle Scenes.
Oliver Wendell Holmes—Weaning of Young America.
George W. Curtis—The Way to Peace.
William Everett—University of Cambridge, England.
R. S. Matthews—The Union.
Theodore Tilton—State of the Country.
Ralph Waldo Emerson—The True American Idea.
Wendell Phillips—National Reconstruction.
Jacob M. Manning—Republican Manhood.
Andrew L. Stone—Campaign Life.
George H. Hepworth—American Patriotism.

THIRTY-SIXTH COURSE. 1864-65.

John B. Gough—Fact and Fiction.
Theodore D. Weld—John C. Calhoun.
Oliver Wendell Holmes—New England's Master Key.
George W. Curtis—Political Infidelity.
George W. Briggs, Salem—True Statesmanship.
Ralph Waldo Emerson—Social Aims.
Wendell Phillips—The Times.
Frederic Douglass—Equal Rights for the Freedmen.
George Thompson—The Amendments to the Constitution.
George B. Loring, Salem—The New Era of the Nation.
Charles G. Ames—The American Experiment.
Thomas W. Higginson—The Freedmen of Port Royal.

THIRTY-SEVENTH COURSE. 1865-66.

Frederic Douglass—The Assassination and its Lessons.
Alonzo H. Quint—Recollections of the Campaign in Virginia.

Edward S. Atwood, Salem—Words.
Ralph Waldo Emerson—Social Forces.
Oliver Wendell Holmes—Poetry of the War.
Thomas W. Higginson—America, Greece and China.
Paul A. Chadbourne—Iceland and the Icelanders.
Wendell Phillips—Politics of the Day.
Richard H. Dana, Jr.—American Loyalty.
Jacob M. Manning—Reconstruction.

THIRTY-EIGHTH COURSE. 1866-67.

Clara Barton—Work and Incidents of Army Life.
James W. Patterson—Revolutions the Steps of Progress.
Frederic Douglass—On Some Dangers to the Republic.
James C. Fletcher—Two Thousand Miles up the Amazon.
Ralph Waldo Emerson.
Charles C. Shackford.
Mrs. F. E. W. Harper—Our National Salvation.
Jacob M. Manning—Samuel Adams.
George W. Briggs, Salem—Frederic W. Robertson.
Edward S. Morse, Salem—Modes of Locomotion in Animals.

THIRTY-NINTH COURSE. 1867-68.

Wyzeman Marshall—Macbeth, with Readings.
Jacob M. Manning—The Coronation of Labor.
Frederic Douglass—Self Made Men.
Theodore Tilton—The American Woman.
George B. Loring, Salem—Colleges and College Men.
Edwin P. Whipple—Loafing and Laboring.
Ralph Waldo Emerson—Eloquence.
Wyzeman Marshall—Hamlet, with Readings.
Adin B. Underwood—Narrative of Campaign Life.
Edward S. Morse, Salem—Social Status of Man.

FORTIETH COURSE. 1868-69.

Wendell Phillips—Daniel O'Connell.
Frederic Douglass—William the Silent.

Jacob M. Manning—Old John Brown.
Theodore Tilton.
Wyzeman Marshall and Miss Lucette Webster—Readings.
Ralph Waldo Emerson—Brook Farm.
Edward S. Atwood, Salem—Across the Sea.
Edward S. Morse, Salem—Art of Illustration.
Henry W. Foote—Notes of Travel in Europe.
George B. Loring, Salem—Jefferson and Lincoln.

FORTY-FIRST COURSE. 1869-70.

H. C. Barnabee and a Double Quartette—Concert.
Theodore Tilton—True Statesmanship.
Mary A. Livermore—Various Reforms.
Frederic Douglass—Our Composite Nationality.
Russell H. Conwell—No Kingdom in North America.
Wyzeman Marshall and Miss Lucette Webster—Select Readings.
James Freeman Clarke—What for?
Ralph Waldo Emerson—Courage.

FORTY-SECOND COURSE. 1870-71.

Mary A Livermore—Queen Elizabeth.
George A. Marden—Hash, a Metrical Essay.
Russell H. Conwell—China and the Chinese.
Gilbert Haven.
J. J. Pinkerton—Sir Philip Sidney.
Wyzeman Marshall and Miss Lucette Webster—Select Readings.
Ralph Waldo Emerson—Hospitality.
Edward S. Atwood, Salem—Mary, Queen of Scots.
George B. Loring, Salem—Distinguished Men of Essex County.

FORTY-THIRD COURSE. 1871-72.

Temple Quartette—Concert.
Russell H. Conwell—Lessons of Travel.

Edward E. Hale—Diary of Mr. and Mrs. Boothby.

Robert K. Potter—The Adirondacks.

Edwin C. Bolles, Salem—Development of Physical Life.

Gilbert Haven—Yesterday and To-morrow.

Wyzeman Marshall and Miss Lucette Webster—Select Readings.

William H. H. Murray—What I know about Deacons.

FORTY-FOURTH COURSE. 1872-73.

Wyzeman Marshall and Miss Lucette Webster—Select Readings.

Russell H. Conwell—Heroes and Heroines.

Thomas Wentworth Higginson—What I saw in London.

Edward S. Morse, Salem—Development by Natural Selection.

Warren H. Cudworth—Up Hill and Down.

John P. Putnam—Passion Play at Oberammergau.

William H. H. Murray—My Creed.

Charles S. Osgood, Salem—Two Expeditions through the Maine Woods.

Carroll D. Wright—Sheridan's Campaign.

FORTY-FIFTH COURSE. 1873-74.

William H. H. Murray—Temperance.

Warren H. Cudworth—What's What.

Russell H. Conwell—A Day in a Lawyer's Office.

James Freeman Clarke—Equilibrium; or how to balance oneself.

Elias Nason.

Edward E. Hale—Read a story entitled "In His Name."

Abby Sage Richardson—Readings.

Wayland Hoyt—Hints towards a Noble Life.

FORTY-SIXTH COURSE. 1874-75.

Wyzeman Marshall and Miss Lucette Webster—Readings

Warren H. Cudworth—"In the Dark."

George B. Loring, Salem—Advancement of Science.
H. M. Gallaher—Put Money in Thy Purse.
S. Lewis B. Speare—Behind Prison Bars.
James Freeman Clarke—Dramatic and Lyric Element in Literature and Art.
Wayland Hoyt—How to Better Things.
W. S. Clark—Vegetable Growth.
William H. H. Murray—Poverty.

FORTY-SEVENTH COURSE. 1875–76.

Wendell Phillips—The American Indian.
Warren H. Cudworth—"Success."
James Freeman Clarke—Imagination.
Sidney Woolett—Readings.
L. H. Angier—Enthusiasm.
H. M. Gallaher—After Clouds, Fair Weather.
George B. Ford—Readings.
Lennon Quartette—Concert.

FORTY-EIGHTH COURSE. 1876-77.

Wendell Phillips—Meaning of the Presidential Election.
Abby Sage Richardson—Readings.
Thomas Wentworth Higginson—How to study History.
J. F. Lovering—The Minute Man and the Volunteer.
Abba Goold Woolson—The Yosemite Valley.
James Freeman Clarke—Kentucky.
Joseph Cook—Ultimate America.
George B. Ford—Readings.

FORTY-NINTH COURSE. 1877-78.

Boston Swedish Quartette—Concert.
William E. Eastty—Readings.
Edward S. Morse, Salem—Japan.
Charles G. Ames—Good Society.
Abba Goold Woolson—Respectable People.
Helen Potter—Readings and Personations.

George B. Ford—Readings.
Wendell Phillips—Charles Sumner.

FIFTIETH COURSE. 1878-79.

George B. Loring and Henry K. Oliver—The Lyceum of the Past.
William Parsons—Michael Angelo
Laura F. Dainty—Readings.
Helen Potter—Readings and Personations.
A. A. Willits—Sunshine.
William E. Eastty—Readings.
Wendell Phillips—Sir Harry Vane.
John Goldberg—Mind Reading, etc.

LIST OF OFFICERS.

PRESIDENTS.

Daniel A. White,	1830-33.	Edward A. Holyoke,	1845-46.
Stephen C. Phillips,	1833-35	George Wheatland.	1846-48.
Charles W. Upham,	1835-38.	Stephen P. Webb,	1848-51.
Abel L. Peirson,	1838-39.	Oliver Carlton,	1851-52.
Henry K. Oliver,	1839-40.	George Wheatland,	1852-54.
John Wayland,	1840-41.	O. B. Frothingham,	1854-55.
Stephen P. Webb,	1841-42.	Richard Edwards,	1855-56.
Charles A. Andrew,	1842-43.	George W. Briggs,	1856-67.
James W. Thompson,	1843-45.	George B. Loring,	1867-

VICE PRESIDENTS.

Stephen C. Phillips,	1830-33.	George Wheatland,	1845-46.
Charles W. Upham,	1833-35.	Stephen A Chase,	1846-48.
Abel L. Peirson,	1835-38.	Benjamin Barstow,	1848-51.
Henry K. Oliver,	1838-39.	Stephen Osborne,	1851-53.
John Wayland,	1839-40.	O. B. Frothingham,	1853-54.
Joseph G. Sprague,	1840-41.	Richard Edwards,	1854-55.
Caleb Foote,	1841-42.	George Andrews,	1855-63.
Jas. W. Thompson.	1842-43.	Albert G. Browne,	1863-67.
Edward A. Holyoke,	1843-45.	James Kimball,	1867-

CORRESPONDING SECRETARIES.

Charles W. Upham,	1830-33.	Richard P. Waters.	1847-48.
Charles Lawrence,	1833-35.	George F. Chever,	1848-49.
William H. Brooks,	1835-38.	Nath'l Hawthorne,	1849-50.
Jona. F. Worcester,	1838-40.	Gilbert L. Streeter,	1850-54.
Oliver Carlton,	1840-41.	Henry J. Cross,	1854-70.
Nathaniel B. Perkins,	1841-45.	Charles S. Osgood,	1870-
Rufus Putnam,	1845-47.		

RECORDING SECRETARIES.

Stephen P. Webb, Jan. 1830 to Apr. 1830.		Henry M. Brooks,	1846-47.
		Amory Holbrook,	1847-48.
Benjamin Tucker,	1830-32.	Joseph B. F. Osgood,	1848-50.
William H. Chase,	1832-34.	George F. Choate,	1850-52.
S. W. Stickney,	1834-38.	Sidney C. Bancroft,	1852-53.
Joseph G. Sprague,	1838-39.	George Andrews,	1853-54.
Henry Wheatland,	1839-41.	Joseph M. Newhall,	1854-61.
Luther Upton,	1841-43.	Henry J. Cross,	1861-73.
George D. Phippen,	1843-46.	Charles S. Osgood,	1873-

TREASURERS.

Francis Peabody,	1830-32.	Stephen B. Ives,	1848-54.
Henry Whipple,	1832-48.	Gilbert L. Streeter,	1854-

MANAGERS.

Leverett Saltonstall, 1830-31.
George Choate, 1830-31.
William Williams, 1830-30.
Rufus Babcock, 1830-33.
Malthus A. Ward, 1830-30.
Abel L. Peirson, 1830, 33-34.
Jonathan Webb, 1830-32.
Rufus Choate, 1830-30.
Caleb Foote, 1830-40.
John Moriarty, 1830-34.
C. Lawrence, 1830-31, 35-38.
Thomas Spencer, 1830, 33, 35.
Henry Whipple, 1830-31.
George Peabody, 1830-31.
Philip Chase, 1830-30.
Henry K. Oliver, 1830-37, 40.
Stephen P. Webb, 1832, 37-40.
William H. Brooks, 1832-34.
Charles G. Putnam, 1832-32.
William H. Chase, 1832-32.
Francis Peabody, 1833-37.
S. W. Stickney, 1833-33.
Benjamin Cox, Jr., 1833-39.
J. A. Vaughan, 1834-35.
Nathaniel Peabody, 1834-37.
Oliver Carlton, 1834-39.
E. A. Holyoke, 1835-39, 43, 47.
John Glen King, 1836-36.
Ferdinand Andrews, 1836-36.
Joseph G. Sprague, 1837-37.
S. A. Chase, 1838, 44, 45.
John S. Williams, 1838-39.
Stephen Osborne, 1838-50.
Jonathan C. Perkins, 1839-39.
N. B. Perkins, 1839, 40, 46.
Luther Upton, 1839-40, 43.
Wm. P. Richardson, 1840-40.

A. J. Sessions, 1840-40.
Samuel A. Safford, 1840-42.
Samuel Williams, 1840-40.
Jas. W. Thompson, 1841-41.
George Wheatland, 1841-44.
Francis A. Fabens, 1841-45.
Joshua H. Ward, 1841-43.
John Wayland, 1841-41.
Oliver Parsons, 1841-45.
Wm. Mack, 1841-46, 57, 58.
Charles H. Pierce, 1841-42.
Thos. D. Anderson, 1842-42.
S. F. Barstow, 1842-46.
James Chamberlain, 1843-47.
Benjamin H. Silsbee, 1844-45.
William Hunt, 1844-47, 51.
Edward H. Payson, 1845-47.
W. H. Prince, 1846-47, 54-57.
George West, 1846-47.
Richard P. Waters, 1846-46.
Henry M. Brooks, 1847-47.
Augustus D. Rogers, 1847-49.
Rufus Putnam, 1847-47.
Henry B. Groves, 1848-50.
Amory Holbrook, 1848-48.
Nath'l Hawthorne, 1848-48.
Wm. H. Thorndike, 1848-48.
Gilbert L. Streeter, 1848-49.
Geo. F. Choate, 1848-49, 52.
Washington Very, 1848-50.
J. L. Waters, 1848-50.
G. F. Chever, 1849-51, 53, 56.
Henry O. White, 1849-50.
Samuel Johnson, 1849-66.
J. B. F. Osgood, 1850-51.
Stephen H. Phillips, 1850-52.
Daniel Perkins, 1850-52.
Neh. Brown, Jr., 1851-52.
O. B. Frothingham, 1851-51.
Henry L. Lambert, 1851-52.
George Creamer, 1851-51.
George H. Emerson, 1852-53.
Wm. D. Northend, 1852-53.
Robert C. Mills, 1852-52.
James Kimball, 1853-66.
Albert G. Browne, 1853-62.
William Chase, 1853-53.
Henry E. Pope, 1853-53.
William Archer, Jr., 1854-55.
Samuel P. Andrews, 1854-66.
Francis Cox, 1854-55.
Willard P. Phillips, 1854-54.
J. Lewis Russell, 1854-54.
George Ropes, 1855-56.
William Silver, 1856-62.
Frederic Winsor, 1857-57.
Israel E. Dwinell, 1858-62.
Jacob Batchelder, 1859-62.
Willard L. Bowdoin, 1859-69.
Alpheus Crosby, 1863-66.
George R. Chapman, 1863-
A. Augustus Smith, 1863-
Thos. H. Frothingham, 1863-
Charles A. Ropes, 1867-67.
John S. Jones, 1867-67.
James O. Safford, 1867-67.
Joseph H. Leavitt, 1867-67.
William P. Martin, 1868-
Nathaniel J. Holden, 1868-
John Barlow, 1868-74.
Joseph H. Webb, 1868-
Nathaniel Brown, 1870-
Henry J. Cross, 1875-

TRUSTEES.

Daniel A. White,	1852-63.	Stephen H. Phillips,	1857-67.
Stephen C. Phillips,	1852-57.	Caleb Foote,	1863-
George Peabody,	1852-	Alpheus Crosby,	1867-74.

Prof. Crosby died April 17th, 1874, and the vacancy thus made in the board has not been filled.

OFFICERS FOR 1878-79.

President.—George B. Loring.

Vice President.—James Kimball.

Rec. and Cor. Secretary.—Charles S. Osgood.

Treasurer.—Gilbert L. Streeter.

Managers.—Thomas H. Frothingham, A. Augustus Smith, George R. Chapman, William P. Martin, Nathaniel J. Holden, Joseph H. Webb, Nathaniel Brown, Henry J. Cross.

Trustees.—George Peabody, Caleb Foote and one vacancy.

ACT OF INCORPORATION.

The act of incorporation under which the Salem Lyceum acts at the present time, reads as follows:—

COMMONWEALTH OF MASSACHUSETTS.

In the year one thousand eight hundred and fifty-two.

AN ACT TO INCORPORATE THE SALEM LYCEUM.

Be it enacted by the Senate and House of Representatives in General Court assembled, and by authority of the same, as follows:

Section 1. Daniel A. White, Stephen C. Phillips, George Peabody, their associate petitioners and successors, and the male citizens of the city of Salem of twenty-one years of age, purchasers of tickets to the twenty-third course of lectures of the Salem Lyceum, are hereby made a corporation by the name of the Salem Lyceum, for the purpose of diffusing knowledge, and promoting intellectual improvement in the city of Salem, with all the powers and privileges, and subject to all the duties, restrictions and liabilities set forth in the forty-fourth chapter of the Revised Statutes.

Section 2. The said corporation may hold real and personal estate, to be used for the purposes aforesaid, not exceeding in all the value of twenty thousand dollars; the legal title to which shall be in three Trustees and their successors, to be chosen by the corporation, at a meeting of members thereof legally called for that purpose.

Section 3. When any vacancy shall occur in said board of trustees, by death, resignation, or incapacity to perform the duties of said office, said vacancy shall be filled by the corporation at a meeting of the members thereof legally called for that purpose. Said trustees shall be subject, in the care, management and disposal of said property to the control and direction of a joint board, consisting of the trustees and board of directors for the time being; which board of directors shall not consist of more than fifteen members.

Section 4. All property now owned by or which may accrue to the Salem Lyceum, shall belong to the trustees before mentioned, subject to the control and direction of the joint board above named.

Section 5. Male citizens of Salem of the age of twenty-one years shall be eligible as members of the corporation, but the corporation at any meeting legally called for that purpose may make such by-laws and regulations in regard to membership, choice of directors, and other matters for the purposes of their incorporation herein before provided, as it may deem proper.

Section 6. This act shall take effect from and after its passage.

Approved April 20*th*, 1852.

BY-LAWS.

The code of By-Laws adopted under the provisions of the foregoing act and now in force, are as follows:

Article 1. Any person eligible by the charter may become a member of the corporation for the year by purchasing a ticket to the annual course of lectures and signing these by-laws, and his membership shall cease upon his failing to purchase a ticket for one year.

Article 2. The board of directors shall consist of a President, Vice President, Recording Secretary, Corresponding Secretary, Treasurer, and eight Managers. They shall be elected by written ballot, by general ticket, and shall hold their offices till others are chosen in their places.

Article 3. A meeting of the corporation for the choice of officers shall be held in the month of May annually. Special meetings of the corporation shall be called by the Recording Secretary when directed by the board of directors or by the written request of ten members.

Article 4. The President, or in his absence the Vice President, or a President *pro tempore*, shall preside at all meetings of the corporation and of the board of managers, and the board of directors, and the joint board of trustees and directors.

The Recording Secretary shall notify all meetings of the corporation and respective boards, and shall keep a record of their proceedings, and he shall be sworn to the faithful performance of his duties.

The Corresponding Secretary shall be the organ of the Lyceum in its conference with other associations and the public.

The Treasurer shall collect and receive all dues and donations and pay all demands from the funds of the corporation, when approved by the President or Recording Secretary, and shall hold all the funds of the Lyceum, except the property invested in the names of the trustees, subject to the order of the joint board of trustees and directors. The Treasurer shall also at the annual meeting, in the month of May, make a report of his receipts and disbursements, and he shall give such security for the faithful discharge of his trusts, as the joint board of trustees and directors shall require.

To the Board of Directors shall be confided the general affairs of the Lyceum, with authority to make arrangements for the delivery of lectures and other exercises, and to devise and execute such measures as may best promote the objects of the association. They shall have power to fill vacancies in their number from the members of the corporation, and to make by-laws for their own government.

Article 5. The Trustees shall be chosen from the members of the corporation and shall hold all the real estate and stocks now standing in the name of the Salem Lyceum; and all funds of the corporation which may be hereafter invested in real estate or personal property and securities, shall be invested and stand in the name of the trustees, provided that the Treasurer shall hold all dues and donations received by him, until he shall have been directed by the joint board of trustees and directors to invest the same or to transfer to said trustees. And said trustees shall hold their offices until they are vacated by death, resignation, incapacity, or removal from the city.

Article 6. A meeting of the joint board of Trustees and Directors shall be held annually in the month of May, or as soon thereafter as may be convenient; and special meetings shall be called at any time when the board of directors or five members of the corporation shall require.

Article 7. At all meetings of the corporation ten members must be present for the transaction of business, but no alteration shall be made in these by-laws unless notice of the intention to propose such alteration shall have been publicly given in two or more newspapers of the city, seven days before the meeting, and unless by a vote of two-thirds of the members present and voting thereon. At all meetings of the joint board, two trustees and five directors shall constitute a quorum. And at all meetings of the board of directors five shall constitute a quorum.

Article 8. All meetings of the corporation shall be called by public notice in two or more newspapers published in the city of Salem, seven days before the meeting.

Article 9. The Trustees and members of the board of Directors shall be presented with a ticket to the course of lectures annually, and such presentation shall be equivalent to the purchase of a ticket for all the purposes of membership of the corporation.

Adopted, *July* 21*st*, 1852.

www.ingramcontent.com/pod-product-compliance
Lightning Source LLC
Chambersburg PA
CBHW021527270326
41930CB00008B/1134
* 9 7 8 3 7 4 4 7 3 6 1 9 0 *